A Journey to Bethlehem

Inspiring Thoughts for Christmas and Hope for the New Year

JASON SOROSKI

A Journey to Bethlehem: Inspiring Thoughts for Christmas and Hope for the New Year Copyright © 2015 Jason Soroski

Visit the author's website at www.jasonsoroski.net

Connect on twitter @Soroski

Second Edition.

Published by Hourglass Ministries, Houston, Texas

ISBN: 1542523362
ISBN-13: 978-1542523363

DEDICATION

To Jana, who patiently encourages me to finish
whatever it is I'm writing.

CONTENTS

Preface   vii

1   A Journey to Bethlehem   1

2   Happy Holidays vs. Merry Christmas (or, Just for the   4
    Halibut)

3   Why I Love Christmas Carols, and You Should Too   6

4   Just Drop the Blanket   9

5   The Rest of the Story   12

6   The Christmas Truce   15

7   The Last Week of the Year   19

8   To Reflect and Resolve   22

9   Resolution   27

10 Christmas Without the Tree   28

PREFACE

What's not to love about Christmas?

Christmas is filled with sights and sounds that make it unique from any other season, and the time that stretches from mid-December to New Year's Day has always been my favorite part of the year.

When I was a kid, it seemed as if that time would slow down while those last few days slowly ticked off the calendar, and then something else wonderful and unexplainable happened yet again when the calendar rolled on into a New Year. It was the sentimentality of closing an old door and the anticipation of opening a new one. As an adult, that fascination remains, and I have done all I can to pass that wonder on to my children, and just about anyone else who is willing to hear about it…

Each December, we embark upon a figurative Journey to a lonely city called Bethlehem, following those familiar steps into the wonder of a newborn King born in a manger so long ago. In my mind it is a tableau of every story I have heard surrounding the birth of Jesus: shepherds, angels, a wooden stable filled with hay, Mary, Joseph and three wise men from the East. Sometimes I imagine there is a light dusting of new fallen snow, sometimes it is rough desert, with only the occasional palm tree to be found.

O Little Town of Bethlehem, you truly are a wonderful place.

There is no doubt that what happened that night in this otherwise insignificant city that has changed the world, but what does it mean for those of us living in the 21st century?

Over the years, Christmas and New Years have been

a frequent topic at my blog The Way I See It. It is a joy to reframe these thoughts into a collection that I hope will not only rekindle the joy of Christmas, but will encourage you to fully embrace that joy and carry it on into the New Year.

When the lights and festivities are over and life kicks back into gear in January, there is no reason for that spirit we call Christmas to fade away, and no reason for our Journey to end, but it is a hope that should carry us throughout the year to come.

1
A JOURNEY TO BETHLEHEM

Christmas.

There are so many things that happen around Christmas that make it the wonderful thing that it is. The familiar songs, the classic movies, the baking, the bright decorations, the festivities and the lights shining from rooftops all across the city are just a few of the things that make Christmas a special time of year. In our family, we have more traditions than we can fit into the month of December!

But there is one that stands out among the rest.

Every night in December we celebrate the Advent season as a family in the run up to Christmas Day. We read Scriptures, sing Christmas songs, talk traditions, and pray together. This year, on the first Sunday of Advent we spent time sharing our favorite Christmas traditions, and as soon as someone said their favorite was the Journey to

Bethlehem, everyone else in the room was shouting, "Hey you took mine!". There is no doubt that the Journey to Bethlehem has certainly become a favorite to everyone in our house each December.

Each year, a local church puts on this "Journey", which is essentially a re-enactment of the familiar events surrounding the birth of Christ in Bethlehem so very long ago. For our family it has become a tradition, and sometimes it seems it would not really be Christmas without it. Complete with sheep, camels, realistic street scenes, Roman soldiers, Wise Men from the East and a host of angels singing Hallelujah, it takes just a little bit of imagination to find you have been transported out of today's fast-faced social media world and back to a distant time and place, to a world crying out for a Savior.

And then it doesn't take long to realize that at its core the world we live in today isn't really all that different from the world of long ago.

Last night we took the Journey to Bethlehem with a group of friends and experienced it all once again. One might think that after a few visits it would grow repetitive and boring, but even after years of hearing this story, and years of seeing it played out, the story never gets old. Even though I am familiar with it and I know the ending, it still evokes the strongest of emotions, it still carries the deepest of meanings, and it still reminds me that there is a purpose to it all.

That somewhere beyond the Christmas hustle and bustle, there lies a child in a manger.

That somewhere beyond the noise, there is a Silent Night.

That Almighty God so loved the world that He wrapped Himself up in human skin to walk among us.

That whoever believes in Him shall not perish, but have everlasting life.

And it occurs to me that Christmas itself is really all

about journeys. God's journey to reach us where we are, the long journey of a man named Joseph and Mary his betrothed, the journey of Magi from a far-off land following a star, the journey of shepherds to 'see this thing that has happened', and the journey of all those who had to travel for the census decreed by Caesar Augustus.

In a symbolic way, Christmas is a journey for all of us too.

A journey out of what is comfortable and from all that distracts us, to a small stable in a small town where the Savior of the world lies resting.

A journey from our everyday life to a remote, ancient, and majestic place where we kneel and worship.

A journey from the cacophony of media we surround ourselves with to a faint cry of a newborn King.

Christmas, it turns out, is a microcosm of life itself, in that it is all about a journey. A journey to something so simple, yet so complex, that we could never fully comprehend it, but instead must learn to accept in faith what lies right before us.

And as I reflect, I realize that this is a journey I should make a lot more often.

2
HAPPY HOLIDAYS VS. MERRY CHRISTMAS
(OR, JUST FOR THE HALIBUT)

For some time the phrase "Happy Holidays" has been the politically correct alternative to the much more archaic Dickensian phrase of "Merry Christmas". Most people don't seem to have much of an issue with it, but we have been told that there is a war on, and all things Merry and all things Christmas are subject to attack. However, secularists beware! Even when saying the less offensive, "Happy Holidays", you still may have unwittingly fallen into a well-laid trap of Anglo-Saxon religiosity. . .

The trap lies in the origin of the word "Holiday". Once upon a time, in the bygone days of the Anglo-Saxon

4

language in England (around 950), the two words halig (holy) and dæg (day) were joined to create the word haligdæg, which was used to describe days of religious observances. The Anglo-Saxons were predominately practicing Christianity at this point in history, so this would have referred specifically to Christian holy days. As the English language changed, the word evolved into haliday around the year 1200, and then into the more familiar 'holiday' somewhere around 1500.

Of course, in our 21st century world we also refer to non-religious days as holidays (Opening Day and Super Bowl Sunday are my favorite examples). Still, at the heart of the word itself there remains the suggestion that we are celebrating something that is "holy". So even the word holiday, at its core, holds a religious significance.

As for the halibut, what does that have to do with anything?

Well, the funny sounding name of this funny-looking fish is derived from the Middle English words hali (again, holy) and the word butte, meaning flat. The fish received this name after it had become a popular dish on Catholic holidays.

Holy flat fish, Batman!

So go ahead and enjoy your holiday halibut, and I wish you and yours a very Merry Christmas and a Happy Holiday!

Oh, and Season's Greetings of course.

3
WHY I LOVE CHRISTMAS CAROLS, AND YOU SHOULD TOO

I spent this chilly December morning at the tire shop listening to Let It Snow.

I was honestly not surprised to find myself there; new construction is plentiful in the neighborhood, and eventually a nail or scrap of metal was bound to find a way into one of my tires.

Awesome.

As I sat in the waiting area, admiring the little Christmas tree, listening to the Christmas music playing overhead, watching others silently sing along, it occurred to me that there is something truly universal and unifying about this thing we call Christmas.

Not only is it so clearly meaningful to Christians around the world, Christmas is a significant part of our national heritage and its presence is felt everywhere we go. In Christmas we find a reflection of who we are as a culture, evident in the number of Christmas movies, Christmas books, Christmas songs, Christmas trees, Christmas candy, Christmas EVERYTHING that surrounds us this time of year. From Rockefeller Center to the local tire shop, the Music of Christmas surrounds us.

In the midst of all this, there is a nostalgic corner where traditional meets modern, secular meets sacred, and a unique blend of all things Christmas comes into view. Pretty much every one of us knows at least a few lines from Silent Night, Joy to the World, White Christmas and Rudolph the Red-Nosed Reindeer. Most of us have never actually roasted chestnuts on an open fire, but the lyric from that song is inscribed on our hearts.

The Music of Christmas is unlike anything else: there are songs that clearly depict the birth of the Messiah (like Away in a Manger) and there are songs that really have nothing to do with Christmas at all (like Jingle Bells). This music fills the airwaves, fills our hearts and fills our collective remembrances, often calling to mind the strong emotions of the season

If you love music, then Christmas really is the best time of the year. It is the one time of year when tradition and singing old songs in a new way are not only accepted but expected! We long to watch movies from 60 years ago, and we want to sing like Joy to the World, O Come All Ye Faithful, and Silent Night, which have been around even longer than those movies. We can package it in the modern, or strip it down to the basics, but the Music of Christmas remains universal.

Why do musicians keep recording Christmas albums? Because we keep wanting to hear them!

At the heart of all of this Christmas music are the Christmas carols. Songs like these have been sung for generations. It is still fun to sing about those who "go a wassailing among the leaves so green" and those demanding that we bring them some figgy pudding before they leave our property. But even more rewarding is to sing songs declaring the birth of the newborn King.

So I encourage you to embrace the songs of this season. When the story of Jesus is being told out in the open from every public speaker, embrace it, and sing Joy to the World at the top of your lungs!

Seriously.

Because the birth of Jesus indeed gives us reason for great joy, and our faith in Him gives us a reason to "Go tell it on the mountain that Jesus Christ is born!"

4
JUST DROP THE BLANKET

It has been over 50 years since "A Charlie Brown Christmas" aired on national prime time television. In a world where the latest greatest technology is outdated in a matter of months, and social media trends come and go in a matter of days, 50 years of anything becomes quite meaningful.

I am a fan of all things nostalgic and all things Christmas, so when the two are combined I am hooked, and the Charlie Brown Christmas special falls squarely into that category.

I was in the first grade back when they still performed Christmas pageants in schools (less than 50 years, but still a very long time ago), and our class performed a version of the Charlie Brown Christmas. Since I was kind of a bookworm and already had a blue blanket, I was chosen to play the part of Linus. As Linus, I memorized Luke 2:8-14, and that Scripture has been hidden in my heart ever since.

But while working so diligently to learn those lines, there is one important thing I didn't notice then, and didn't notice until now.

Right in the middle of speaking these words, Linus drops the blanket.

Charlie Brown is best known for his uniquely striped shirt, and Linus is most associated with his ever-present security blanket. Throughout the story of Peanuts, Lucy, Snoopy, Sally and others all work to no avail to separate Linus from his blanket. And even though his security blanket remains a major source of ridicule for the otherwise mature and thoughtful Linus, he simply refuses to give it up. Until this moment.

When he simply drops it.

For the first time I noticed that in that climactic scene when Linus shares what 'Christmas is all about', he drops his security blanket, and I am now convinced that this is intentional. What convinced me is the specific moment he drops it: when he utters the words, "fear not".

Looking at it now, it is pretty clear what Charles Schulz was saying through this, and it's so simple it's brilliant.

The birth of Jesus separates us from our fears.

The birth of Jesus frees us from the habits we are unable (or unwilling) to break ourselves.

The birth of Jesus allows us to simply drop the false security we have been grasping to so tightly, and learn to trust and cling to Him instead.

It is during this speech that Linus is telling us, "what Christmas is all about", and he even throws in a visual for effect.

The world of today can be a scary place, and most of us find ourselves grasping to something temporal for security, whatever that thing may be. Essentially, our world today is a world in which it is very difficult for us to "fear not".

But in the midst of fear and insecurity, this simple cartoon image from 1965 continues to live on as an inspiration for us to seek true peace and true security in the one place it has always been and can always still be found.

5
AND NOW, THE REST OF THE STORY

That beautiful moment when Linus 'drops the blanket' is a beautiful and meaningful moment that has been hidden in plain sight for 50 years. When I first wrote down that I noticed it, I had no idea that the response would be so overwhelming. That moment has become a topic for Christmas Eve messages across the world, and an encouragement to numerous people wrestling with fear and uncertainty.

As a pastor, I am thrilled at the encouragement it has given, and as a former literature teacher, I am thrilled that it has started a firestorm of film analysis! As so many people have now begun to dig deeper into this scene, many of you have pointed out that at the end of the scene Linus picks the blanket back up, and have wondered why.

It makes sense to ask about it. Why is it, that after the epic, blanket-dropping recitation of Scripture given by Linus in response to Charlie Brown's quest for meaning, he picks the blanket back up.

Isn't that anti-climactic?

Why would Linus pick that security back up after so boldly proclaiming an end to fear? Why does he leave the stage with that security blanket still in his hand?

We first must realize that we all carry that same blanket.

Just like Linus, we may stand tall in a moment of faith and conviction. A moment when Scripture hidden in our heart comes to life, and we fling all else aside as we experience and proclaim the true freedom and security that only Jesus can give.

But at some point, out of habit, we reach down and pick that thing right back up.

Faith is powerful, but it is also delicate.

Linus clearly knows the truth, clearly proclaims the truth. The knowledge is there and the wisdom is there and the passion is there. So why does he pick the blanket back up?

I think the answer is strikingly clear. It is because we all do that exact same thing.

We know. We feel. We proclaim.

Yet we gaze in the mirror one morning to find that tattered old blanket is draped back over our shoulder yet again. And we realize that we have become so used to it being there that we hardly even noticed.

It is rather discouraging to think about, actually.

But the good news is that the story does not end there.

The story ends with the Peanuts gang gathered around the Christmas tree and singing. It is here that they realize, 'it never really was such a bad little tree', and it is now glorious and beautiful. Yet even now, they are not just singing, but clearly and unquestionably singing in worship, first quietly and then loud and boldly. Even the musical style at this point is strikingly different from anything else previously.

The obvious song choice here could have been "O Christmas Tree", which has already been playing gently in the background. Not to mention they seem to be singing about the tree.

But the song changes here because we realize the focus is no longer the tree. The focus has become bigger than the tree.

The focus now is Jesus.

With this new focus, the kids now slide effortlessly into singing "Hark the Herald Angels Sing, Glory to the Newborn King! "

What we are now witnessing is essentially an impromptu cartoon worship service.

But before any of this happens, Linus parts with that blanket yet again. This time he lays it down for good at the base of that beautiful Christmas tree. This also tells us something: just as Linus tossed that blanket down somewhere nearby only to pick it back up again, he finally lays it down at the foot of the Christmas tree. Perhaps the lesson is that we should forever lay our fears and anxieties at the foot of the cross.

Linus and the others have moved from *hearing* truth and *speaking* truth into a deeper place of worship, where they finally *respond* to that truth, much like those shepherds who were told to "fear not" so very long ago.

It is here that Linus lays that blanket down yet again, and this time he doesn't look back.

6
THE CHRISTMAS TRUCE

Peace on Earth.

Christmas is a time when we celebrate the coming of the Prince of Peace. On the night Jesus was born, a host of angels sang, "peace on earth, good will towards men" and that angelic proclamation has echoed majestically through the centuries.

The Savior of the world arrived as a child, and He arrived in peace.

In spite of this, centuries later wars continue to be waged all across this globe of ours.

World War I, or The Great War was considered 'the war to end all wars'. Of the sixty-five million who fought in this conflict, half never made it home. At the end of this war it was widely thought that after experiencing the devastation and aftermath of modern warfare, humanity would take every measure to prevent it from ever happening again.

Sadly, it was mere decades before the seeds of another World War were sown.

But in the midst of the bloodshed, there is one bright spot that shines out through the darkness of this conflict - the Christmas Truce of 1914.

The Christmas Truce was a brief moment of sanity, a moment in which enemy combatants truly embraced peace on earth, and good will towards those they were supposed to hate.

It was a moment when the men in those cold, muddy trenches soon realized they had more in common with one than they had differences. There is an important lesson for us in that.

On Christmas Eve of 1914, the German troops were seen lighting candles, setting up spruce trees, and singing Christmas carols in the trenches on the Western front. The English troops, in trenches just yards away, could hear this going on and started singing carols in response.

Before long, the Music of Christmas caused these enemies to emerge from their trenches, meet cautiously in the middle, and soon find themselves celebrating an unofficial peace on earth.

Letters from soldiers who were there recall that event, and tell the story of how both sides agreed to not shoot at one another the following day, which was Christmas Day.

These letters describe this unique Christmas. One English soldier who is now unknown to history, but whose letter has survived wrote the following:

"This will be the most memorable Christmas I've ever spent or likely to spend: since about tea time yesterday I don't think there's been a shot fired on either side up to now. Last night turned a very clear frost moonlight night, so soon after dusk we had some decent fires going and had a few carols and songs. The Germans commenced by placing lights all along the edge of their trenches and coming over to us—wishing us a Happy Christmas etc. They also gave us a few songs etc. so we had quite a social party."

Bruce Bairnsfather, who served throughout the war, wrote:

"I wouldn't have missed that unique and weird Christmas Day for anything. ... I spotted a German officer, some sort of lieutenant I should think, and being a bit of a collector, I intimated to him that I had taken a fancy to some of his buttons. ... I brought out my wire clippers and, with a few deft snips, removed a couple of his buttons and put them in my pocket. I then gave him two of mine in exchange. ... The last I saw was one of my machine gunners, who was a bit of an amateur hairdresser in civil life, cutting the unnaturally long hair of a docile Boche, who was patiently kneeling on the ground whilst the automatic clippers crept up the back of his neck."

It is even reported that these enemies gathered the bodies of those who had been previously killed on the front lines, helped to bury them together, and held joint funeral services in their honor.

Being Christmas, some of the officers were sympathetic to this peace. However, other officers were not as pleased, and throughout the course of the war as the battles grew more bitter and violent, commanding officers began to order heavy artillery strikes on subsequent Christmas Eves just to prove their point and keep this kind of thing from happening again. This moment of peace early in the war did not bring an end to the conflict, but it remains a beautiful display of what is possible when people choose peace, and this display lives on in the stories passed down from those who were there.

According to those firsthand accounts, there was a vibrant soccer match played between the two sides that day. The Germans won that friendly match 3-2; the game ended when the ball was kicked into a barbed wire barricade and went flat.

There's a sad symbolism in that.

However, it was a brief moment when peace defeated war.

It was a glimpse of what should be, in the midst of what should never be.

It was a celebration of life, in a world plagued by death.

It was hope in the midst of hopelessness, and light in the midst of darkness.

It was peace on earth, good will towards men.

In short, it was Christmas.

7
THE LAST WEEK OF THE YEAR

Christmas is a time of remembrance.

The season guides us to reminisce about the joys and sorrows of years past, filling our days with favorite movies, nostalgic treats, thoughts of cherished loved ones, and stories from the old days, all swiftly swirling around an ancient story of a baby born in Bethlehem on a silent night. Those defining moments of the past bring us clarity and comfort. Yet while the Christmas lights still glow from rooftops and town squares, the calendar marches on to the 26th, then the 27th, then the 28th until we find ourselves shifting gears, moving in a new direction with a new focus at a different pace.

We leave behind that time of year where our eyes are focused pointedly on the past, and lift our gaze towards the uncertain promise of what is ahead. The familiar sounds and surroundings of Christmas Past give way to the brimming but uncertain blurriness of Future.

The Last Week of the Year, those precious days nestled between Past and Future, are strikingly Present, and allow us that rare opportunity to breathe in the air that is no longer the Old Year, but not quite yet the New.

For most of us, each year brings new hope and blessings, but also brings its fair share of change and disillusionment, our news feeds filling up with heated opinions of politics and religion and culture and every trifle imaginable.

Which makes me realize that we spend so much of our precious time on things that ultimately aren't all that important.

We argue about trivialities until we lose focus and become spread thin.

We become frazzled, angry, ineffective and discouraged.

We go to bed at night realizing that we are somehow missing out on the things that matter and waking up in the morning overwhelmed before we even start the day.

These problems aren't going away on their own anytime soon, and there will be plenty to distract and deter us in every New Year. With the promise of what is new, there certainly will be old struggles that follow us in the journey. But as the lights and decorations come down and the world continues on at a new pace, the same promise of hope we spoke of at Christmas still remains bright and tangible in January as much as it is in December.

The last week of the year gives us a moment to prepare for what is coming. These last few days where Christmas starts to become a distant memory can become an opportunity to pray, plan, and prepare.

These days give us opportunity to not only make meaningful resolutions that will carry us into a new day, but to make a renewed commitment to lay our burdens down and entrust our days to our Father in Heaven.

It gives us a new chance to, "Be still before the LORD and wait patiently for him" (Psalm 73:7).

It gives us a clear opportunity to "Be careful to do as the LORD your God has commanded you; you are not to turn aside to the right hand or the left"(Proverbs 5:32).

Fighting off the ever-present tendency to be distracted and tossed about by whatever the world is throwing at us, the New Year can truly be a new start, a year of reinvention, determined focus, and change for the better.

Certainly there is nothing magical about the flip of the calendar, but it represents a clean break, a new hope, and a blank canvas.

May this Last Week of the Year be a defining moment that refocuses our energies and clears all that is peripheral, until all that remains is all that matters.

May this year be the year that our hearts and minds are filled with wisdom instead of rashness, patience instead of impulse, and forgiveness instead of bitterness. We can do it if we use this last week of the year to get a head start.

8
TO REFLECT AND RESOLVE
(A REMEMBRANCE OF NEW YEAR 2015)

As the world entered 2015, I couldn't help but reflect on 1915.

It was the year Alexander Graham Bell made a phone call from New York to his friend Thomas Watson in San Francisco; the first phone call ever made across the American continent.

It was the year McCrae published 'In Flander's Fields'.

It was the year the US National Advisory Committee for Aeronautics (NACA) was created. It was eventually renamed NASA.

It was the year the planet Pluto was photographed for the first time.

It was the year the Lusitania was sank by a German submarine.

It was the year Woodrow Wilson became the first President to attend a World Series game.

It was the year Henry Ford's assembly line manufactured the one millionth Model T.

It was the year Teddy Roosevelt urged us to avoid being "hyphenated" Americans.

It as the year the Ku Klux Klan was chartered, and the year Jack Johnson was the first black world boxing champion.

Although so much has changed, in many ways the world of 1915 is glaringly similar to the world we inherited in 2015.

The world of 1915 was a world at war. It was a world filled with mistrust between nations, stark political and cultural divisions, and rising racial tensions and misunderstandings. But it was also a world brimming over with promising and innovative new technologies such as the automobile, air travel and voice communications that continue to define our lives a century later.

In 2015 we were presented with another New Year and another set of resolutions. We will yet again slide into another year, resolved that things will be different once the new calendar is hung.

Last year I resolved to read through the Bible in a year. A resolution I kept.

This year, I add to that by resolving to read one chapter of Proverbs a day each day of this year. I started to do that this year, but didn't stick with it. This year I'm putting that at the top of the list of priorities.

This year I resolve to read a chapter of Proverbs faithfully each day, and I invite you to join me. It can only make us better, wiser, and less apt to repeat the mistakes of the past, but rather to chart a new course to better understand and respond to the maddening events that swirl around us.

I pray that this year my heart and mind will be filled with wisdom instead of rashness, patience instead of impulse, and forgiveness instead of bitterness. Each New Year will hold its own challenges, sure. But it can be our best year yet if we are willing to put in the effort. The future history of this New Year is ours to write.

9
RESOLUTION

Webster defines the word as being "marked by firm determination".

The word dominates every New Year's Eve. Each year we resolve to change careers. Get healthy. Make new friends. Earn more money. Be patient. Be assertive. The list goes on, and in just a few hours we will walk through the same old ritual once again.

To the musician, a 'resolution' is a harmony line moving from a dissonant tone (one that does not fit the melody) to a consonant tone (one that fits). Harmonies can dance and amaze us with varied complexities for a while, but they must eventually resolve.

To the writer, a resolution is the end of a story, the final element of a twisting plot wrought with conflict, finally pulling together to an ending where all is well.

To the chemist, it is the separation of a chemical compound back into its constituents, or simplest parts.

To the statesman, it is an expression of the determined will of an elected body.

To the graphic artist, it is the sharpness of the pixel count on a screen, and the quality of the image produced.

By any definition, a Resolution is characterized by a return to order, a focus on sharp definition and determination broken down to its simplest, most harmonious parts.

Without Resolution, art, science, government, and life in general all fall into chaos. Without resolution, there is no foundation on which to stand.

And so, out of the lights, parties, vacation and glory of December, we walk our resolutions back into the bland porridge everyday chill of January.

Out of the joys and regrets of the last 365 days, we have the chance to embrace a new, corrected, and more detailed path for the next lap around the Gregorian calendar.

For some of us, New Year Resolutions are a glaring exercise in futility, as we come back to watch the ball drop in Times Square, and realize we have the same resolutions as last year.

And the year before . .

And the year before . . .

And so New Year's Eve, pregnant with opportunity, often gives way to regret for opportunity missed.

You know, it's really time to change that.

This year I am striving to fix my resolve on simpler things.

I am resolved to be a better husband. I am resolved to write more. I am resolved to learn more about things I don't know. I am resolved to show the love of Christ without condemnation. I am resolved to grow and learn as a parent. I am resolved to be healthy in heart, soul, mind, and body. I am resolved to listen more than I speak. I am resolved to think more about those who are suffering, and less about my daily inconveniences. I am resolved to be content in all circumstances. I am resolved to do life better.

I have wanted these things in previous years and have fallen short. In previous years I have failed to see the big picture. In previous years I became overwhelmed, bitter, discouraged. I have had enough of that. Life is both fragile and fleeting. I refuse to slide into the back half of my life on cruise control. This year I am choosing to live life more abundantly. This year is not about wanting to do better. This year is about making it happen. This year I accept nothing less than firm resolution. When the hoopla is over, when the days begin to settle into routine, this year will be different.

This year, I am Resolved

10
CHRISTMAS WITHOUT THE TREE

Well, here we are. Back to January and back to Ordinary. Back to work, back to school, and back to life after the Holiday hustle.

Bah. Humbug!

Tonight I walked down to the end of the driveway and I felt a certain sadness tugging at me. You have probably felt it too. A holiday chill lingers in the air, but the glowing wreaths, snowmen, manger scenes, ornaments and candy canes that had adorned our street days ago are now all but gone, a few procrastinators notwithstanding. The lights that glimmered, danced, and illuminated the night are now packed away in the garage for another year, and the world is back to normal. Back to plain, dark, and ordinary.

Just ordinary. According to the church liturgical calendar the 12 Days of Christmas are quickly followed by a time called Epiphany, and then the time until Lent is known simply as 'Ordinary'.

Wow. Really?

Just . . . Ordinary?

I guess ordinary is the best way to describe this time of year, but ordinary can still be a good thing.

If you are like me, you have seen some version of *A Christmas Carol* more than a few times. After his visits with the spirits Ebenezer Scrooge makes a big promise: "I will honour Christmas in my heart, and try to keep it all the year." Which sounds great, but what does it mean? Does it mean keeping up the lights? Does it mean keeping up the tree? Does it mean keeping the Rudolph nose on the car and going-awassialing among the leaves so green in the middle of February?

Well….maybe.

But it is more practical to keep Christmas by viewing life through a lens of eternity. We keep Christmas by refusing to forget the miracle of God in a manger.

By considering Christmas as more than just a day, but a mindset; a way of life.

By learning to number our days and seek wisdom as we go.

By allowing that wisdom to forever change who we are.

By choosing to be polite and giving and charitable when we don't feel like it.

Especially when we don't feel like it.

By seeking peace on earth, good will to men.

By starting and ending each day with a prayer of thanks, and by doing unto others as we would have done unto ourselves.

By allowing the spirit of Christmas to invade ordinary and forever change it into something new and better until ordinary takes on a new meaning and Ordinary becomes a fulfillment.

Ordinary becomes joy.

Ordinary becomes sharing cheer and wearing a smile and speaking joy when no one else knows why.

Until Ordinary becomes the same as Christmas, just without the tree.

If we can do this, then what we consider to be ordinary will soon become something extraordinary. Ordinary will become joyful, celebratory, meaningful and filled with purpose. The days that drag on will instead rush past us with the wonder of Christmas, the wonder of Christ. Each and every day will become a day to celebrate, to share, to love and to live a life focused fully on the love of Christ. And that is the way I think we would all prefer to live.

ABOUT THE AUTHOR

Tapping into his experiences as a worship pastor, educator, husband, and homeschooling father of five, Jason Soroski enjoys relating poignant stories from real-life experiences. Writing in a voice that is both insightful and accessible, Jason communicates in a way that is mindful of the small details that we may otherwise overlook in our everyday lives.

In December 2015 Jason wrote, "Just Drop the Blanket; The Moment You Never Noticed In A Charlie Brown Christmas". This encouraging observation went viral and stirred up a national conversation about Christ taking away our fears.

Jason holds an M.Ed. from Missouri Baptist University, is a worship pastor, Christmas enthusiast and regular contributor to crosswalk.com. But he most enjoys spending time with his family, taking road trips, playing guitar and going on new adventures whenever he gets the chance.

Made in the USA
Monee, IL
29 November 2020